Missing,
Presumed Unread

Tom Bryan

Indigo Dreams Publishing

First Edition: Missing, Presumed Unread
First published in Great Britain in 2015 by:
Indigo Dreams Publishing
24, Forest Houses
Cookworthy Moor
Halwill
Beaworthy
Devon
EX21 5UU

www.indigodreams.co.uk

Tom Bryan has asserted his right under the Copyright, Designs
and Patents Act 1988 to be identified as the author of this work.
© Tom Bryan 2015

ISBN 978-1-909357-84-6

British Library Cataloguing in Publication Data. A CIP record
for this book can be obtained from the British Library.

Designed and typeset in Palatino Linotype by Indigo Dreams.
Cover design from Chagall's Four Seasons by Ronnie Goodyer
at Indigo Dreams
Printed and bound in Great Britain by 4edge Ltd
www.4edge.co.uk
Papers used by Indigo Dreams are recyclable products made
from wood grown in sustainable forests following the guidance
of the Forest Stewardship Council.

to Michael and Anna

for my wife, Lis

Acknowledgements

None of the poems in this collection have been previously published.

Thanks to all my friends and family for their time and encouragement. Special thanks to Eileen Gunn and Steven Cook of the Royal Literary Fund in London, whose crucial support has allowed me to find time to write.

In memory of the late Gavin Wallace whose kind and practical support to many writers in Scotland made a vital difference to their careers.

With special thoughts for the late Christina Phillips 1949-2013.

Previous poetry collections by Tom Bryan:

Wolfwind (Chapman, Edinburgh, 1996)

North East Passage (Scottish Cultural Press, Aberdeen, 1996)

Redwing Summer (Selkirk Lapwing Press, Selkirk, 2005)

Rattlesnake Road (Dionysia Press, Edinburgh, 2006)

Doubling Back (Dionysia Press, Edinburgh, 2011)

Until the Roof Falls In (Indigo Dreams Publishing, 2012)

CONTENTS

PART ONE: Sassafras Boy

SASSAFRAS BOY

We pulled sassafras striplings in Spring,
their leafy Trinity pointing our way.
Bark was good but we sought roots.
Cut to cigar size. Sun-dried
until they turned orange, peeling like sunburnt skin.

The smell? Rich earth, rain---maybe a hint of Germolene.
Fill a deep coffee can. Then door-to-door.
But the old people bought while we learned to sell.
"Spring Tonic. Rheumatism. Impetigo. Diarrhoea.
Constipation. The Conquer Root."
An elderly man claimed it even restored his "mojo",
buying four bundles with a grin, at fifty cents each.

But when these folk died our art died with them.
We were the last of the front porch sassafras sellers.
In those towns, it is simply not done anymore.
(No one is left who'll buy the ancient lore)
I too am one of that vanishing cadre,
soon beyond all remedy and cure.

DOCTOR DAVID

He came down from Chicago's Jewish community
to our picket fence town. On holiday,
but stayed. His surgery backed on to his sugar peas,
tomatoes and pumpkin vines.
More than diplomas adorned his reception walls.
Tarnished baseballs, photos of gangsters like Capone and
O'Banion. As a young medic, he rode the ambulances,
learning what a Thompson sub-machinegun could do to soft tissue.
I was once concussed by a baseball. He lectured me, bat in hand
how to evade a curve ball.
"Plant your right foot, step left, like a waltz.
Don't *dive* into its flight path, *klutz*. Here take some tomatoes home
to your mother." He told her to let me sleep. "If he dies, he dies."
He laughed then winked.
My friend Linda recalls his needle breaking off in her arm.
"See what happens when you squirm." (she hadn't)
Soon afterwards he retired to his beloved
vegetable patch.
We often thought of that lonely Star of David
above his oaken door. We later learned that
humour and wisdom also cured:
 it wasn't just pills and vaccines
we went there for.

FLEENER STOLE SOME BEER...

Then just took to the woods, his domain.
Cops left him to it, knowing he wouldn't remain
forever, but would skulk like a squirrel in a hickory tree.
Sensing no further fun in the chase, he
drank some of the beer, that backwoods man
(but only half a can)

Left the beer with a note in some roadside weed.
"Returning 'beer'. Sorry I stole it. Tastes like peed-
on –by- tomcats. No crime to steal
something worth nothing. No big deal
for the pain of that half tin. I'm the fool.
So lawmen, on this hot day, keep cool.
I thus return the beer.
I'm sincere,
Fleener."

FOLK LORE

Turtle, like a small walnut,
all jaws and carbuncles.
On a dare I proffered the tiny alien
my pinkie knuckle,
he took – and how!

He crunched with my every move,
my blood against a whitening bone.
His eyes like starry glitter,
opened and closed, at leisure (his).
Water plunges, lighter fluid, tears.
Nothing worked.
Ah. Old neighbour. Veteran of the Somme.
He'll know turtles.
"Son, them musk turtles
never let go until dusk." (it was noon)
"Gonna have to cut it off"

Turtle or finger? Winking,
he took two pen knives from another era,
blunt backs of both, between skin and jaw.

Deft twist, left then right,
reptile fell unharmed, hissing to the grass.
"You're lucky son, supposing I wasn't around?
Be more careful next time!"

There was never a next time
for turtle or war veteran.
But I have often since twisted things sideways,
prising for a better look.
No hurry. We always have until sundown.

GOING WEST

They had room for me on their summer porch
where velvet moths bulged the screen door
for the light within, waking me from
my western dream.

A man who fought from the Bronx to Vietnam---
and knew mountains, gave me a handgun.
What for? Bears?
"Bears are fine" he said.
"It's people who rattle your head. Take it."

But that revolver lazed under a pillow
while I never managed mountain or sea.
The weapon may be there still,
where moths fly from the dark,
find that light is not their lack
pause gently, unfold---
then return to black.

IN PRAISE OF CABINS

Cedar walls, guns, fishing rods.
 Lake of loons, pike,
perch and walleye.

Scullery, mushrooms, berries and nuts.
Wood everywhere outside and in,
always a fire.

To complete a cliché,
in hectic Spring

mosquitoes flattened calligraphic,
to the rafters.
Raccoons of summer, and jays
rasping in the sun.
A blade of geese.
Then Winter, when the walls groan
and the hard slog until snowmelt comes.

Ok, there must be a beard
and rotgut whisky. Self-destructive thoughts,
conspiracies and somewhere under a
mocking galaxy
a total unravelling.
Prop open the door,
put everything outside.
Clean the chimney, clean the hearth.
Skillets, notebooks, jigs and spinners...
Dust, clean polish and yes, burn.
Then watch the cabin breathe again,
watch its lungs go in and out.
Put things back where they belong,
if shrine, then so be it.
But no clutter within.

Make sure the pump works.
Get fresh water.
If there is hate, it is time to burn it.
Hear me well.
If there is love, it is time to earn it.
Meanwhile, tell
death and the tax man
to go straight to hell.

ISAAC DORMAN
(A black man killed with white troops at the Battle of the Little Bighorn)

This "black white man" maybe didn't want to be here
fighting men whose language and kin he knew.
But honour has as many shades
as the colour of a man's skin.
Wounded, he shouted *goodbye* to a sergeant.

Lakota accounts recall the man they
called *Buffalo Teat,* perhaps a mispronunciation
of his name or the texture of his hair.
It is said Sitting Bull himself gave Dorman a last drink
of water, commanded his warriors not to torture him,
that Isaac sipped then died.

WHAT ELSE JIM DIDN'T TELL HUCK

A schoolgirl biologist found some shark teeth
in her swimming pond. *Fine fossils* she thought,
  but experts said:
"*These* teeth aren't fossilized."
Somewhere up in Dylan's
North Country Fair
thousands of miles from any sea.
How did they get there?
Then they found ten foot
bull sharks swimming in her quarry.
Up from the Gulf of Mexico,
up the Mississippi, but these
man-eaters were Minnesota-born,
freshwater reared. Global warming's
love children.

When I was nineteen, I swam in the Mississippi
not far from there, rope tied to a raft.
I felt immortal, even with the river sucking
at my ankles, currents deep cold and strong.
Ghosts of Huck and Jim, lolling nearby.
"Hey Huck honey, don't move. Don't look behind you.
But pole this raft like hell!"

PART TWO: We Must Remain

"WE MUST REMAIN UNTIL THE ROOF FALLS IN"
Weldon Kees

He remained all right, in a clown suit, head
full of chemicals, singing, speaking in tongues,
called us the audience "losers and cretins."
The price of genius? asked one. *No thanks* some replied.

He eroded his body and mind
 "just for the experience *man*"
then snapped his executive briefcase shut
 for good and played some blues.
His roof fell in but he just kept playing.
And the last song of his last set:
"I'm gonna take to the Highway won't you lend me your
name?"

APOLOGIA
"What nourishes me also destroys me" on Marlowe's portrait

She wins praise being thin (ultra)
too old for catwalk or pinup,
clacking, skeleton walking.
Eyes deep in her head,
a coffee balanced, her only meal
for a day or two.

What does she really think of us,
well fed, we must take too much
of her barely breathing space?

I understand our fleshly threat
when *lean* has the moral high ground.
But hunger also consumes itself,
chews its own muscle, finally gnaws its own vitals.

We wear our weakness for all to see
but your enemy is deeper, within.

CREATIVE WRITING AND WORSE

Murderers and arsonists
gave me poems and stories,
for encouragement and comment.
No **666** on the forehead,
no eyes too wide apart.
Your auntie might even trust them
for scones and tea.

So next time you reckon
he was so polite, cut his grass
minded his own business
was a good neighbour,

Carry this little poem around with you
in case of emergency.

DEPRESSION RONDEAU

My blues drip down like freezing rain.
Can't even sleep and dream again.
Then drop by drop, December sleet.
Rain on a homeless beggar's sheet.
It's time to wake then face the pain.

A blues question, a blues refrain.
These old dragons are never slain.
I'd like to rise, get on my feet.
My blues drip down.

No way to catch a midnight train.
No cash to go to sunny Spain.
I hardly want to drink or eat.
Blues grow cold but I need some heat.
If this won't stop, I'll go insane.
My blues drip down.

LITTLE SOPHIE

Halleluiah!
Little Sophie is writing poetry
wanting to *grow up* to be a *poet.*
(but can you do <u>both?</u>)

Oh wee Sophie, my credit card is full,
3p left in my adult piggy bank.
Heirlooms to sell.
I put some old books in a plastic bag,
(that £100 will do) will tide me over.
Emails accruing, phone ringing.
Power will be cut shortly.

I'm too busy working to have a job (Kerouac)
Writing? Now that's not *too* bad.
But Sophie, please shun poetry,
it makes you go blind
and makes you sad.

MY MILITARY "SERVICE"

I was measured, weighed, whilst coughing
had my testicles squeezed,
torch up my backside. Ears probed, blood pressure
taken. "Intelligence test" passed too easily.

You'll do. Any other questions?
"Since I don't want to kill or be killed
I'd rather not---go, I mean."
He narrowed his eyes, sanitized his instruments.
Nobody does.
Not even the effin enemy.
Next.

But in a week the war was over.
I guess they'd all heard I was coming!

NAMING THE GENERATIONS

First, the *Baby Boomers, Boomers* for short.
Includes me. Last radio, first TV. Cars, polio
vaccine. We maybe hunted and fished, lived
outdoors. Adults skulked in a parallel universe,
smoking, working 9-5. We too like our time-
keeping, had the first and/or too much of everything.
Second, our first children, the X generation.
A bit less a bit more.
More indoors, computers, less space, less freedom,
But rooms of their own.
Third, Y.
Blinds drawn, the mole people.
Texting, thus evolving huger thumbs. Growing eyes
luminous like something from the Marianas Trench,
beginning to quarrel with our planet, practise
skills for something further apace.
Millennials. Post Millennium, post, 9:11, post Jihad,
post Bengal Tiger and Polar Bear? Post global warming.
Practise bidding adieu to our weird rituals,
our primitive skills. Farewell to the Elders and their
strange totems. Not appropriate for these post-Galactic palettes.
Blasting off, over and further out.

OLD MAN TALKING TO THE TV SCREEN

Your boyfriends do not interest me,
or why you would cry yourself to sleep
over Identikit boy A, B, C, or D.

They aren't worth the trouble
or any amount of fitful sleep.
Wash the makeup from your chin
and join the revolution. - or get *them* in.

AK47s will give them bigger hard-ons
than you ever did in bed.
So forget pretty Lance or Dwayne
and what they wrote or should have said.

There is still much work to do.
In the countryside they need
water, food and land.
Only later (maybe) love songs too.

PAID POLITICAL BROADCAST

What can I say about it?
Sleeping four to a room,
two siblings to a bed,
is shit.

So at the soiree I look for an escape
to avoid reminding you
or your pinup politician
that *everyone* should be
clothed, fed, housed, educated
kept healthy, given a minimum income.

That if you say anymore about school fees
holidays in Barbados or your summer homes...
Quick. My coat. I'm ill. It may have been the smoked salmon
or just perhaps the company I shouldn't keep.

PROCRUSTEAN

Fat swarthy innkeeper, unkempt.
Flatulent, never with a willing woman.
Then he had a better plan.
Lost weight, bought a hairpiece.
Shaved more often, used unguents.
Fresh underwear every day,
new clothes. Took elocution lessons,
learned etiquette, learned to tango.
 Had new dental work.
Was ready.

The bedroom decor would be perfect too.
Flickering lamp, laundered bed linen,
hint of lavender in the room.
His guests? The men who used to mock him.
If manly toes were short of the bed end,
a winch would
crack cartilage,
tear tendons and shinbones,
stretch the body frame to fit.
But ah, if more rarely too long for the bed,
a cleaver and butcher's chopping board,
 job neatly done.
Attractive antique bowl to catch the blood,
 all colour-coordinated.

Damaging a thing to force it to fit,
or shrinking it, merely to suit.
Mythical Procrustes showed us all
how it was done
with his *special* bed...
yet
what he did I am still doing...
in my Procrustean head!

SIXTIETH BIRTHDAY

Chekhov did not marry until late,
"fearing the loneliness of it."
That drizzling awareness of self and other,
that chasm curve of sleeping back,
eternal inches from your belly.
Eyes brim, harsh translations from blank stares,
frowns, fear of speaking or of silence
or doing, saying the wrong thing.

I wear what war veterans call the *horizon look.*
Like the harpooner Queequeq's on learning his fate.
Meanwhile, my Black Dog howls,
sensing weakness, easy prey.
I can think of only a few escape routes.
Tawdry, cowardly, painful all the same.

Crusoe was never more lonesome
than *after* Friday came.

WINTER IT IS PAST

No more poems are really needed
about trees and flowers,
French cafes, sunrises, moons.

I see daffodils
and doves flourishing in equal measure,
with impetuous Spring coming,
lovers kissing, a winter reported missing.
Like my friend, now gone for twenty years,
not seen or heard.

Dead maybe
but silence is not what poets do.
April, ever a singing month
tells me to let my winter go.

PART THREE: Multiple Scars (for my wife Lis)

Note: Multiple Sclerosis is Latin for "many scars" referring to the lesions that are formed when the nerve insulation, myelin, is destroyed, leaving scars. These are often seen on brain scans as lesions, characteristic of the disease. There are at least four varieties of MS, differing in severity.

FIRST SIGNS
(Multiple Sclerosis---but we didn't know it then)

Freckled daisy and buttercup lanes.
Fritillaries, dragonflies. Cobalt sky,
trout lying deep, cool.
Then, you fall.
 No, more of a *crumple*.
You *crumple* into the tall grass,
scattering a cloud of micro-creatures
like pollen. You sit there, so
human and small my love, under that
great blue unblinking sky.
Whelped onto the grass,
an exotic, from only god knows where.
I sit beside you.
Youthful hikers also offer help
but yet you lie.
Long minutes later you rise, toddle a few paces.
Crumpling again near the otter hide.
An aerial view? People cluster like daisy petals
around a blonde woman, daisy centre,
fragile amongst azure butterflies.
And a bewildered man
 his hand like a wounded bird,
hovers, hesitant, no place to land.

MULTIPLE SCARS
(MULTIPLE SCLEROSIS)

Get the clichés out of the way.
Battle scars.
Scar tissue.
Scarred for life.
Emotionally scarred.
Scared (sic)
That'll do.
By the way,
clichés are true.

MULTIPLE SCLEROSIS METAPHOR: RAT IN THE FUSE BOX

A rat gets in the fuse box.
Pisses, shits and sperms there.
He especially likes the savoury
taste of insulation, salt on his fissured tongue.
Bites through some, strips some.
Some wires are untouched.
Some lights will flicker,
some will short out,
others function as normal.
But the bedroom light
works in the bathroom.
The kitchen light works in the cellar.

Rats outlive the fuse box.
Nobody knows how to kill the rats.
Nobody knows how to replace the wiring.
The rat appears more knowledgeable
than the electrician.
Feed medicine to the rat to divert
him from his luscious insulation.
Sometimes a hungry rat dies,
giving some breathing space until the next rat arrives:
(there will always be a next rat).
Nobody knows when the next rat(s) will come.
Nobody knows why some fuse boxes are tasty to rats and some aren't.
Or, when the electrician will be born
who can read the diagram and restore the wiring.
Or when an exterminator will come
who will kill all the rats.
Hail, the Pied Piper of Multiple Scars,
we wait, at your mercy.
But please hurry.

MS METAPHOR: CUCKOLD

Someone is running a hot tap on my loved one's nerves.
Molten slivers, searing glass.
Fatigue: like two marathons,
too tired to rise or sleep.
A sumo wrestler has her round the waist.
He tires, a rock python takes over.
Off is on, off is of and fo,
on is off, o, n and NO.

Worse, my love is in bed with another.
A disease.
He uses her. Does all he wants.
A shape shifter, craven coward,
won't come out and fight,
back door monkey man,
ravages her all the time,
has her in thrall.
Takes all, gives nothing
but pain.

MS METAPHOR: DISEASE AS BUREAUCRAT

Have you seen that vigilante man? I been hearin' his name all over the land. Woody Guthrie.

Hello, I'm Mr. S. O'Path
from the Department of MS.
I'm here for the *screw you* assessment.
We'll not take your car,
just your ability to drive it.
Our largesse allows you to keep your food and wine,
we'll just repossess your ability to taste and chew it.
I'll let you keep your poetry and drama
but take away your ability to use a pen
or computer.
We'll keep reassessing. Our department will never stop
serving you...up. And keep on taking
and taking, until you drop.

PART FOUR: Still Travelling

STILL TRAVELLING

York Station, a bench, platform three.
"Still travelling" dedicated there.
Welcome wood in all this plastic
In Memoriam between train and me.

The epitaph is a compelling one.
Still travelling? Travelling is life,
what better place than the mainline?
(Dead at thirty-eight, she was much too young)

Here the King's Cross train is in your face.
This quiet seat on the firing line.
Pigeons and one robin bob for crumbs.
Tannoy: *when boarding, please mind the space.*

Minding space, many don't pause there.
Fast food seems a desecration.
Maybe water, juice or coffee
but in time, memorial transmutes into chair.

Weekly, I return here.
Scan any seated pilgrims who don't see
the carved wooden mouse--- climbing
trademark of this bench maker.

Two drunks argue to the Middlesbrough train.
Angry men with briefcase battering rams.
Blind man clicks with a white-tipped cane.
Grey women in trainers, infants on reins.

London train arrives, faces blankly bright
with mobile or laptop, like decals on a toy.
It's time to rise. My own train is late.
Rough wind down the concourse. Freezing night.

Filtering daylight will change the mood.
Dust motes clear with morning.
Station thrums to the rush hour.
A cleaner polishes the thirsty wood.

Late, early, broken down, can't run.
We on this bench are grateful just to be.
Still travelling is her memorial
but ours too, until our last train comes.

AT YORK UNIVERSITY

Greylags stutter in the parking lot.
Canadian Geese strut their white chinstraps
down a student catwalk. Laminated posters identify
Shelduck, Barnacle and Coot.

Do hungry scholars assay
variations on goose fat recipes,
stir fry or crispy duck pancakes,
from what waddles down the Cycle Way?

Yes, I do like the waterfowl,
despite the fouling, the smell,
the unprovoked attacks,
that garrulous mating call.
An old drake defends his lifelong mate
against taxi and delivery van.
Awkward on asphalt, graceful in water,
blusters nowhere on comic feet.

Fresh poetic ideas are nascent, overdue
on this energizing stroll to lunch.
Tiptoeing poet and truculent drake---
 both more graceful in some other milieu.

ARGO STREET MELBOURNE

On the way past a golden cupola,
fretwork houses not made of gingerbread,
but festooned with lemons
and birds belonging to rain forests.

An armful of yellow roses, plus falafel
and Japanese cherries,
moon glinting from the Russian Orthodox Church,
above which Orion
hangs perfectly upside down.

WARBURTON, VICTORIA, AUSTRALIA

This is more like it: my Australia of the mind.
Yellow wooden house, cosy porch,
blistering under a same-coloured sun.
Spiders as big as table coasters.
Cockatoos stealing apples from
scolding rozellas.

First glimpse of *bogan* culture,
tattooed, potbellied, satisfied.
Parrots, trout farms, butterflies,
vegetable stalls, crickets and jungle sounds.

The small dog will go
only so far, his comfort zone
ends with the grassy outback,
where dreamtime begins.

FOUND NEWSPAPER POEM, AUSTRALIA

"England wins – honestly this is not a misprint."

"Shock! Horror! Poms win."

It's not (just) cricket.

DESERT ISLAND DISCS

Fish hook, line, knife, bandage, aspirin.
Matches, purification tablets, the clothes I'm in.
Maybe a brain seeing only what a slug
feels or snail sniffs. Somewhere warm
without snakes. Nobody looking for me
just yet, missing presumed unread.
A few poems bubbling in my head.

THE CLEVER ONE: ISTANBUL HOSTEL, 1976

The male bunkroom was full but we heard it all next door.
Through thin walls, he had some pot then offered her some.
They weren't English but spoke English.
I think he was Turkish, she French.
"You are so cleever (sic)" she sighed and toked.
With each fresh puff, they kissed and petted,
laughed, panted, moaned, and screamed.
She sang out on reaching climax.
We could have clapped, were silent.
Soon, they started again.
"Oh, oh, you are so *very very cleever*" she half-
exploded, and again and again
 until the dawn muezzin finally drowned her out.
Meanwhile,
we couldn't offer the stoned chanteuse
anything at all. Our collective useless hard-ons
wilted in the sultry heat.
Through the thin wall, we could almost see
and hear the ultra cleever one
smirking at our sullen jealousy.

LAST SPEAKER OF BO

Andaman Islands. She died, the last speaker of Bo.
Folklorist and linguist had bled her dry,
filled their files and CDs,
memory sticks with nobody left to translate.

An old woman who could only
speak to herself, answer her own
questions. Who began to taste her final words
like a weaning infant.

Bo's Rosetta Stone?   Tiger Shark in a blue lagoon?
A chambered nautilus?
Mermaid's purse?
What's left after an overnight typhoon?

PART FIVE: Wolf Dream

FROM WOLF DREAM ALBA

This long mainly unpublished poem, "Wolf Dream Alba" is set on top
of that stunning mountain Suilven in Sutherland. The poet camps on
the summit in the last days of the last millennium. Part one has
previously been published. Part two appears here in print for the first
time. Wolf Dream Alba is a long meditative poem in ten parts.

Part Two
"Morning"

The salmon vision

That night the wind shifted,
down from Cape Wrath,
hail slapped the tent, ice formed
on the fly sheet. Snug in my sleeping bag,
I dreamed, drifted....

Dreamed of ice in great wedges,
groaning up the Strath,
birds and fish starved,
hills melted into acid pools.

This was repeated, like a newsreel,
thatch burning
skeletons falling into ditches.
Nettles, reeds and bracken
flourishing where corn and oats once grew.
Black ships rounding the headlands,
keening to the wind
the wind hushing their song.

The day was dark, the tent darker.
My vision darkened with it.
A land choking in grease, fags and lager,
a merciless rain of fitba and Prozac,

soap opera cliches.
Tea, more sugared tea
in front of wally dugs and electric fires.
Cardigan cultures, skag and shag.
Clogged arteries, lacerated kidneys,
high blood pressure and piles,
magazine pictures of the Royal Family
mounted above the mantel.
The *New* Scotland on Millennium Eve!
And a slave (Scotsman)
And a slave's slave (Scotsman's wife)
and a slave's slave's slaves (his children)
punching, gouging, battering,
frae Maidenkirk to Johnny Groats---

Whaur's mah tea, bitch?

In the name of Pilate or Christ,
I see clearly the lighthouse of Stoer
but we need a bigger beacon than that.

Me and my nation, screwed, chewed and tattooed,
from Cape Wrath to Cape Clear,
from hell to Texas and here,
domestic horrors, mental tortures
phobias, delirium tremens
heroin joneses: all in picture postcard land,
mair like BRIGADOOM
where upper-class twerps
shoot their blanks, Ante-Bellum,
while in the byre, fank and field,
calloused hands rub mojos
from hell to Quinag.
Hyphenated tax dodgers exercise feudal
rights on their great hectares of stag toilet.
Apologise for the Clearances?

They're no finished yet!

I've seen desperate escapes.
From rooms lichen-damp.
They leap out on knotted ropes
(they are doing it now).
One way, no return,
a white trash past-time.
It is cold, so cold, when the slates rattle
and the bed is lonely.

So come the thrushy May,
I will go a'leaping,
with a hey and a heck
and a rope round my neck.

And I have cut them down,
Lord knows, I have cut them down.

*   *   *   *

The sun rose, the wind softened,
the lochs were a sparkling latticework.
Eden was beyond me, hope beyond Eden.
Fionn Loch, a gash of slender
birches mark the Falls of Kirkaig,
where the great salmon leap and fall back,
into pools at this world's end.

(Memory)

One late summer on the Kirkaig,
down the rock staircase
(to the bottom ledge)
people return from the Falls,
claiming no salmon are there.

Yet watch the slate surface, the spume, the spray,
silver runs, argent leaps,
the falling and sinking,
downstream to willow pools.

Slow worms and adders on the path,
chanterelles like orange peels, amanita
and agaric, birches delicate and peeling,
hoodies croaking---then---
one silver leaper
gasping on a bed of moss.
My vision and memory restored
by the breathing poetry of that awesome fish.

Cho fallain ris a'bhreach (so healthy as a salmon)

Alba?

From the yolk and safe liquid,
into the world's din and roaring.
An eerie wash and drizzle
among the detritus of plant and mineral.
Food for trout and cormorant,
perch and pike, eel, stoat, rat and mink,
otter and angler.

(Seven herring a salmon's food,
seven salmon a seal's food)

Infections of liver and swim bladder,
poisons, acids, virus and bacteria,
on the journey from golden yolk to silver fish.
A fierce will, deep in the blood and tissue,
deep in the cells, a silver coat
of armour against the sea.

A quickening of river and cloud
and all the shadow creatures above and below.
Salt in the eyes,
on the tongue, nipping scale and gill.
New shapes and outlines, gull and gannet,
different jaws waiting, different deaths.

From peat-dark pockets of pool,
slender- reeded, gentle parasol of water lilly
and algae, to the cold morgue of sea horizons,
no shores, only night cannibals and horrific
sea creatures, far from gentle birth and birdsong.

Youth---fish or man, more energy than fear,
sleek muscle, reddening flesh, vice-like jaws,
leaping under sun and moon, away from
bigger jaws, into vast seas.
Great leaper--- salmon of wisdom,
eater of hazel nuts in the great pool
at the world's end, mystery fish,

symbol:

heroes in wolf skin and bear fur
sought seven times seven years,
slew seven times seven dragons,
won seven times seven maids,
seeking a fish eating hazel nuts.

(the modern reality is different)

Finn and Cuchulainn do you
seek salmon bloated by chemical pellets
in fibreglass pens and cages,
rubber-fleshed muscle,
among fungicides from hatchery to sea

all needs provided,
food, safety, medical care,
swimming circles of sickness.
Easy pickings for heron and stoat,
lobotomised under dark lids....Symbol?
I gave you one.

(the journey over the sea)

We leave
out from Glasgow, Edinburgh, Dundee,
from bothies, slums and tower blocks,
frae the fairm toons and dreich toons;
over the sea.....

And a winter died on Suilven
mist smooring all light below
and my daylight vision ended
with that great Diaspora,
emigrating, keening, young and old,
the sea only a wider pool.

Cha til, soraidh leis, mo shoraigh leis...

some never reach the river
never reach the sea
never reach the further shore
and…some never return.

I dipped my cup into the pool
and drank until my head ached.
while the Wolfwind snarled and hissed.

(the vision of the Shaking Tent)

My mind cleared,

a waterfall of light
bathed my brain.
I saw the ritual of the "Shaking Tent."
Translated from the Inuit, The Sammi,
the reindeer tribes:

the seeker must go to the tent,
for his tribe and his people, in times
of famine, blight, moral unrest.
He must go in deep humility.
He must be empty.

The tent is a Mississippi Crossroads
where bargains are struck
and minds bartered.
The novice or charlatan is driven insane,
battered by reason and unreason,
returns from the tent broken, deranged,
or visionary.

An Inuit told a Cree
who told an Assiniboine,
who whispered to a Gael
who whispered to me:

to the tent voices come,
howling song or unclear whisper.
The tent shakes, spins,
the ground beneath is rent,
connecting the molten earth
to the sky.
Energy passes through the tent
then the dreamer has new eyes,
he flies over the earth,
talks with the dead,
finds the body of the drowned fisherman,

the missing suicide.
But never for himself alone
but for the people, the tribe, the nation.

I had drunk only water
and only tea made from pure water
for two days.
Slaked, I entered the shaking tent,
a lamb to the wolves.

A STONE (MORE OR LESS)

You wouldn't see it from the road,
from stile or fence.
Mist is the visual default,
or a blackbird where bracken
rusts and rots.

You may be too tired
to test the barbed wire
this dreich day, but let your
wellies squelch, just further,
through a ribcage of birch.

A standing stone four thousand years upright,
perfectly split in two by ice.
We're told *lunar calendar, sun marker, compass.*
The archaeological high ground, spiritual,
resolute.

But why not just two Stone Age teenagers
in cave bear hoodies, bored?
A reckless bit of graffiti, upended vandalism,
on the way downhill, a rave to celebrate
that retreating winter?

The petty, the banal, the senseless
vapid drizzle of every single day.
This is how we connect, how
humans understand. Like finding
dice made from mammoth bones.

"This was their casino, their
youth club, a place where people
merely hung out".

Tribes too jaded or canny
to worship monuments, ravens or solstices.
If we really don't know why
those stones are *here*,
then let's think *outside* the circle.

FABLE FROM A SOUTH LANARKSHIRE SCRAP YARD

"**Jesus**" he said, rolling a fag.
"They told me to *clear* the site.
Take it all away.
So I did. Good industrial scrap,
metal for the market.
God, how many nails do imperialists need?
It was mostly crap. Roman maybe,
but still rubbish.

But the *expert*s intervened.
Archaeological treasure trove.
They came with fancy boxes and labels.
Secretly I kept some, gave some away."
He held three nails in his
rust-stained palm.
Pointing one towards his wrist.
He continued: "A two thousand year old
spike--- fit for purpose.
Imagine *this* hammered *into* you---
Christ!"

MOUNTIE JAMES MACLEOD CONFRONTS SITTING BULL, SASKATCHEWAN, SEPTEMBER 1877

Red Coat, a Skyeman,
Turned the name slowly on his tongue:
"Ta tanka-I-yotank", *Sitting Bull.* Holy Man,
prophet, warrior, now refugee in Canada,
Illegal immigrant. MacLeod was warned
the Hunkpapa Lakota
could read a man's soul.
MacLeod was tired
that September in the Cypress Hills.
He could smell winter, remembered other meetings,
other blizzards, lone white man among the tribes.
Where were those warriors now?
"Isapo-Muxica", Crowfoot,"
"Mekaisto," "Redfoot" "Pitikwahana"
of the Cree?
Treaty Number Seven at Blackfoot Crossing.
"We trust only the Redcoat"
Said Blackfeet, Cree, Assiniboine.

MacLeod grinned. Maybe his red coat *was* potent.
Brilliant vermillion, easy for arrow or sniper,
scarlet souvenir for any brave.
Maybe this General Custer was merely
an arrogant Yankee, child-killer,
glory seeker?
But this Sitting Bull? MacLeod's Cree Scouts
said could stop Red Coat's heart with one glance.
But the Red Coat admired Sitting Bull's
taste in hideaways.
Wolves, bandits, buffalo and Lakota came here.
MacLeod knew this land's Cree name:
"myun-a-tuh-gow" *Beautiful Highlands.*
MacLeod sniffed the dust,

Heard the grasshoppers quivering,
sensed scorpions and kangaroo rats.
Overhead, geese flew south.
Red Man and Red Coat breathed the dying perfume
of late summer. Blue flax, wild pinks,
yellow sweetclover, carmine.
Both men breathed the musk of bobcat, wild turkey,
moose and dying buffalo herds.
The white man's own memory danced on prairie dust.
Drynoch, Skye, oceans and dreams away.
Beinn Bhreac, Roineval, Glen Varragill.
Fifteen hundred people cleared in two decades,
leaving only two sheep parks.
Joseph Mitchell said of Glen Drynoch:
"nothing was heard by the passing traveller
except the bleating of sheep."
Now, MacLeod sees the Sioux camp for the first time,
Repeats his mantra, his orders, slowly.
OBEY THE LAW, NO TREATIES, NO RATIONS,
GO EASY ON THE BUFFALO,
YOU ARE GUESTS IN CANADA.
Eyes meet, gazes held. Red Coat's is a hard justice.
But *these* Highlands will not be cleared.
Human speech and song can bide a while
with scorpion and coyote.
These Lakota will not be evicted.
Hunkpapa Prophet praises this Red Coat
for his justice and mercy.
MacLeod's work was finished,
watching the sun die on the living hills.
He thought again of Glen Drynoch,
and the bleating of sheep,
people scattered, winter coming.

METAPHOR FOR THE PAINTED PEOPLE

But where did the dark men go, caught in crossfire
between Berserker and Gael?
Foe from both mountain and sea,
bloodaxe and claymore.
Time for metaphor?
A flag, a tricolour? Red for blood
and the Norsemen beards.
Green for the Gael, up from leafy Argyll.
Blue for the Picts, the painted ones,
but their blue strip in the middle
is thin, wavering, a fading tattoo.
A trio? A choir? Three languages in dissonance,
then later a duo, raucous, battle-loud.
Three religions, then two.
A sandwich, with nothing in between the bread?
A vice, with only blood in its jaws?
A cloth dyed with three colours,
mixing blue with green and red?
What's left--- a dovetail, a mosaic, an original blend?
They will tell you in Wick
they are purely Norse,
in Thurso that they are mainly Gael.
Yet the dark painted ones had no voice in this.

Maybe once on the Plains of Cat,
along that boundary on The Burn of East Clyth,
those indigenous folk saw only slavery east or west,
hostage to the flesh markets of Constantinople
or swineherds for a Gaelic chieftain,
beyond their known world.

They put down their spears, refusing to fight or run.
Then chanting, changed into Ravens
and flew to the sun.

Leaving their foes glowering only at each other,
over a blood-red burn,
fearing what had flown but would never return.
Then both tribes turned and fled
behind the invisible wall
which yet stands.

Gallaibh. The Gaelic word for Caithness, "land of foreigners, strangers."
Probably the Gaels describing the Vikings.
Caithnessians are still called "Gollachs" today.
"On the east side of it (The Burn of East Clyth) scarcely a word of Gaelic was either spoken or understood, and on the west side English shared the same fate..."
George Davidson, Minister, Latheron, 1840.

SCOTLAND AS MOSAIC

Red hair. World-wide, becoming rare.
Hair like my mum's, a real Scot.
From Viking, Gael, Irish, Angle?
From Isobel, Jessie, Elspet?

Mitochondrial DNA (in my spit)
says it may have come 8000 years ago:
 the Ket Tribe, a nearly extinct Siberian
hunting, gathering lot.

Mum's forebears crossed ice bridges
 to hunt Neolithic creatures *Here*.
Moral of this incomer's tale?
Scottish Mosaic is *Magic*. So *There*.

LETTING GO

My cold lumpfish cadaver,
gurney-bound,
to a medical school, where
vapid students smirk at
my shrunken penis, liver spots
varicose veins.
Prodding, wisecracking.
Then, after a time
(and I have plenty of time)
eulogies are said at
a cremation. Ashes returned to
next of kin.
Let the task begin.
Please put the dust in a big pepper mill,
(the kind Italian waiters
anoint carbonara with)
A giant salt shaker also serves.
Or, I'm a grandfather, so why not a snuff box?
Ready?

Oh aye, Celtic Park. 'Paradise' is good.
Do it under the floodlights, half time
during a big match with Barca or Juventus.

Shower some in the Abhainn Mhor,
swallowed by golden trout at spawning time.
 From an open canoe on Veyatie and Cam Loch.
Pepper some over the adders of Suilven,
feed the young ash tree roots I planted
in our Field of Thorns.
 Also *wherever* chanterelles grow.
(Aye, an IKEA pepper mill holds a lot!)

Scottish Borders? Dust Selkirk and Kelso, strew

some atop The Eildons.
Float a fistful on the ramparts of Berwick-on-Tweed
on the last day of July,
followed by a fish supper.

No mote must remain
nor on any mantel stand.
Let loose all
in any place once loved by me
(when I wasn't dust, when I wasn't free)

Indigo Dreams Publishing Ltd
24, Forest Houses
Cookworthy Moor
Halwill
Beaworthy
Devon
EX21 5UU
www.indigodreams.co.uk